Anna Sproule

The Role of the Media

Macdonald

A MACDONALD BOOK

© Anna Sproule, 1986

First published in Great Britain in 1986 by
Macdonald & Co. (Publishers) Ltd
London and Sydney
A BPCC plc company

ISBN 0 356 11618 2

Editor Donna Bailey
Production Controller Rosemary Bishop
Picture Research Elizabeth Loving

Printed in Great Britain by
Purnell Book Production Ltd
Member of the BPCC Group

Macdonald & Co. (Publishers) Ltd
Greater London House
Hampstead Road
London NW1 7QX

BRITISH LIBRARY
CATALOGUING IN PUBLICATION DATA

Sproule, Anna
    The role of the media. – (Debates)
    1.Mass media
    I.Title II.Series
    302.2′34 P90
    ISBN 0–356–11618–2

Contents

What are the media?

Until this century, few people talked about the media. They talked about the press instead, since the press and the main medium – or means – of mass communication were one and the same thing. But starting with the development of photography in the nineteenth century, the methods by which information could be passed on to a large audience changed dramatically.

When radio, and later television, joined the tools at the communicators' disposal, the size of the audiences involved grew to an extent previously undreamed-of, and the term 'media' was coined to cover the whole contents of the information industry's tool-bag.

The media of today Television has now ousted the press as the most powerful mass medium. Potentially radio still has an even wider reach, but its impact is more limited than that of its younger cousin. The cinema, though historically of great importance, is today in the throes of being eclipsed. The same eclipse has been confidently predicted for the principal written medium, the newspaper, but it hasn't happened yet. Meanwhile magazines are also surviving in large variety, while the number of books published increases year by year.

Too much power? The modern media, both electronic and printed, touch our lives at almost every turn. They keep us informed

War news, racing and what the stars foretell: as shown by this display on a New York newsstand in 1943, the media meet a wide variety of daily needs for information and entertainment, in a wide variety of languages.

'They tell me my product is commercial – as if that's something bad. I think that's fabulous, I love it.' *Judith De Paul, US television executive in Broadcast, 1986*

Stooping to overcome an obstacle: the media's newsgatherers wait to get pictures of the French agents who in 1985 were jailed for their part in blowing up the Greenpeace flagship *Rainbow Warrior* in New Zealand.

...nd they keep us entertained; they exert normous power over what we know, what ve think, and what we feel. Any institution which wields power on such a scale is a natural focus for criticism. This book examines the role of the media in modern ociety, and considers the most important question of all: are the media too powerful?

What sort of control? Different countries have different ways of handling the issue of media power. Totalitarian countries, for example, fully recognize this power, and employ strict controls to ensure that the content of what reaches their citizens will not lead to social or political unrest. When the disastrous fire broke out in the Chernobyl nuclear reactor in April 1986, the Russian media machine only made the news public two days after the event, and then only as a result of pressure from the countries affected by the radioactive cloud. Normal Russian news stories concentrate on positive aspects of Russian life such as raised production figures for factories; however, ordinary Russians are aware that they're being kept in the dark.

State control of this order is abhorrent to the democracies of the west. But other controls exist here which are just as limiting to the media's scope. The most important one stems from the fact that newspaper and television production in the west is a business, often a very big business. It exists to satisfy a commercial demand, to please the consumers at the other end of the production line. If it looks as if something won't achieve this aim, the word goes out 'Kill it.' The consumer may never know what's been left out.

Which set of controls works best? And which carries the greater justification?

'Whenever the evening television news comes on, most viewers walk out of the room.' *Russian newspaper quoted on BBC 1, 1986*

What makes

The best story in the news today is the one that was read first by the newscaster on television. Tomorrow morning it will be the one that gets the biggest, most obvious headline on the first page of a newspaper. Often the story chosen by the newspaper for its page one lead will not be the same as the television one, not because events have moved on, but because the things that make good press stories and those that make good television ones are not necessarily the same. Television is a visual medium, so a good story here has to have the possibility of good pictures attached. Newspapers are less limited in this way. But in spite of such technical differences, all good news stories have certain features in common.

Information: who needs it? Since news consumers in the west are free to choose what they want to watch or read, media people feel fully justified in making sure that everything they do is geared to giving the public what it wants. They agree that the public wants information, but more importantly, people want to be interested, not bored: they like to have people they

can look up to; they also like to have people they can despise, even hate. They like excitement and drama, even if the events shown to them are not particularly pleasant. A story on hospital resources for example, will have a good chance of being used if it features cancer patients or children threatened with death because of lack of equipment. A story about geriatric patients, the acknowledged 'poor relations' of western medical care, rates less highly in news terms.

At the same time, however, people don't like their most deeply-held values and preconceptions to be upset. It worries them an acknowledged villain-figure of the social scene is shown in a sympathetic light. the same way, they prefer an issue to be outlined in clear terms of black or white since this makes it easier to absorb. It also makes it more dramatic.

A story that meets some or all of these needs is, by the media's own standards, good story, even if its information content is low. In the widest sense, the media are in the entertainment business rather than the information one.

The story – or the truth? It can be argued that since the media have such enormous power, they should be more responsible about the way they use it. A news item should be a faithful description of the facts irrespective of its 'story' value. Reality, the argument runs, is too important to mess around with, and a story goes on being true, and therefore worth considering, even after it has been dropped from the headlines.

People also feel that the media should at least attempt to lead public taste rather than merely reflect it. Some facts – the geriatric patients in a seedy hospital, for example – are too difficult or too boring to illustrate for television. Does that really mean that audiences should remain ignorant of them?

One of the biggest television stories of all time was the public death of the seven Challenger astronauts. In news terms it had everything: pictures, high drama, shock, victims with whom viewers could identify. For the astronauts and their families, the tragedy cannot be minimized. But bigger groups of people die frequently; why do the media not give them the same – or more – coverage? Could it be because their deaths are not sufficiently 'entertaining'?

a good story?

People like happy endings
to stories, so a happy ending
is a good story in itself.
As the QE2 steams into
Southampton with survivors
from the Falklands war, the
camera records the joy of
the waiting relatives and
friends.

*'One cannot show an interesting picture of a
man thinking. What you will see is Princess
Diana accepting a bouquet.'*
Brian Walden,
TV presenter and journalist, 1985

All the news

that's fit to print?

It's rare for a politician to make an important public speech off the cuff. Normally the speech exists well in advance as twenty or so pages of typescript, which it will take the speaker half-an-hour to read out. It's obviously impossible for either the electronic or printed media to publish the whole speech, or even a substantial part of it, since it's just one item among many on the news editor's list. The news machine therefore has a choice: either to print a highly condensed report of the speech, covering all the points made, or to concentrate on just a few of the speaker's topics, maybe even on just a few striking sentences. The more sophisticated the news handlers, the more likely they are to choose the second option.

Abridge – or distort? Anyone who reads or watches a news account of an event they've witnessed may well be surprised at the effect that comes across. It's recognizably the same place and the same people. But the witness is often left with the feeling that 'it wasn't quite like that'. Drastic cutting has changed the whole character of the event.

Again, people who are in the news often complain that their remarks have been distorted. This too is often the result of cutting. Indeed, it is possible to turn the facts completely upside down while still appearing to be accurate. A politician, for example, could say 'There is a widespread belief that the economy is on the upturn. Though as yet there is little tangible to support this view, such figures as are available don't disprove it.' As reported, this statement could emerge in one of several ways: 'The economy is on the upturn'; 'Little to support upturn theory'; 'Minister dashes economic hopes'; or 'Minister cautiously optimistic'. Which condensed version comes closest to what the politician really said?

What do they get paid for? Most people have neither the time nor the inclination to sift through a mass of detail before getting to the facts they really want to know. There is no reason why they should; sorting and reducing information to manageable proportions is what a journalist gets paid for. Another part of the job is interpreting the information received. 'Minister dashes economic hopes' might, in fact, be the right line to take, given what the reporter knows about the politician concerned.

Shrinking world, expanding problem
With the explosion in telecommunications, information is an industry that is expanding all the time. News comes pouring in to the news desk from further and further away: from different countries, different continents, even from space. So the pressure on television time or newspaper columns is not going to get any less; it's going to increase. Many people would say that the distortion risks involved in cutting material are an acceptable price to pay for easing the problem. They might add that the subjects of news stories, although quick to complain about the way the media treat them, are the last people to be able to judge the value of what they've said.

Opposite Patient, regal, stylish, domineering: the four faces of Raisa Gorbachov, wife of the Soviet leader, produced in under five minutes by one of the commonest techniques of presentation used in newspaper work. Which of them is the real Raisa – if any?

'The camera which cannot lie photographed that which it looked for.'
Anthony Smith in The Politics of Information, 1978

'Members of the public have this strong idea that what they read is true, rather than it being just an attitude to the facts.'
Andrew Marshall, co-author of Fleet Street TV series Hot Metal, 1986

Subversive

Whatever means they use for the purpose, all the mass media are capable of reaching huge audiences quickly. It is really this that gives them their great power, a power that becomes greater still when it is linked with their ability to present attractive and easily understood images. Television, radio, and the press are all enormously effective tools for changing readers' and viewers' opinions, life-styles, political attitudes and moral values.

Powerful institutions inspire fear, and from earliest times the media have always been regarded with varying degrees of suspicion by the public. In particular, they arouse suspicion in authority figures who fear that their authority may be by-passed or undermined. This suspicion is expressed in accusations of everything from causing disease (via infected cinema seats) to subverting the rule of the state.

When printing, the technology behind the first mass medium, was invented, its use was very strictly controlled. In Britain a heavy duty was often payable on newspapers, and journalists had to fight hard to win the right to report the proceedings of Parliament. (The debate over the right to televise the proceedings of Parliament is still continuing.) In the United States of America, the situation is rather different. US authorities have traditionally taken a liberal view of the media's role in society and the US public's 'right to know' is enshrined in the First Amendment of the constitution. Totalitarian countries, however, take an entirely opposite view and exert tight censorship over what the media report.

Best left in the dark? Many people feel that some things are best left uncommunicated. Perhaps these deal with topics that are distressing, such as animal experiments conducted for medical research. Perhaps they deal with topics that are 'sensitive', that deal with people's deepest emotions and that, handled ineptly, could do great damage. Religion is one such issue; another is a person's ethnic origins. Other things that people (or the law) feel should be left unsaid include details of military installations and, on the grounds that it might lead to panic, possible threats to the public's health and safety.

The power of the mass media in the 1930s: the language of a Chicago mobster sounds odd in the mouth of this little old lady.

"You see what they're doing, Emily? – Taking him for a ride. Presently we shall see them sock him and possibly bump him off."

'Congress shall make no law . . . abridging the freedom of speech, or of the press.'
First Amendment to the US Constitution, 1789

agents?

The power of the mass media in the 1980s: two children are transfixed by the moving pictures in their kitchen. Both cinema and television have been the focus for frequent attacks by people who envy their ability to hold attention and alter behaviour.

A crucial role? An opposing view is that the public has a right to know about anything that concerns it. The media, far from being an institution to be feared, are of crucial value in a free society, since they are the main agents through which the public can be informed.

Commentators on the Russian media system point to the way it has both done its public a disservice, and discredited itself, by exercising such a tight control on negative news. When the Russian liner *Mikhail Lermontov* sank off New Zealand in 1986, the Russian media stayed silent on the subject for over a day. They eventually handled the story, but on their foreign news service only. 'Its deafening silence', commented Mary Dejevsky in *The Times* shortly after the *Lermontov* sinking, 'on accidents within the Soviet Union has allowed Western agencies to score propaganda points by being the first to inform the Soviet public of accidents in their own country.'

> '*Soon there will not be room enough in the same country for the monarchy and The Times.*'
>
> *Prince Albert (1819–1861), husband of Queen Victoria*

A threat

Children under 15 are among the keenest of all television audiences. Both in the United Kingdom and the United States, they watch something like five hours a day.

They also spend something like five hours a day in class at school. In terms of time alone, teachers and the media are equal competitors for influence over a child. When the media's goals conflict with those of education (and sometimes even when they don't), the media can be seen as at least a potential threat to what teachers are trying to achieve.

Wider horizons? Young children in a remote country district of Britain recently watched a television programme in school on the British textile industry. The programme was set in an industrial town in the north of the country, and many of the workers shown were women whose families originated in India and Pakistan. None of the children had ever met a Commonwealth immigrant and at first they were bemused. Why was the programme about Britain when the people in it were Indian? Their teacher, however, used their bewilderment as a starting-point for a discussion on the growth of Britain's multi-cultural society. With the help of the programme, she could fill in a gap in the children's knowledge.

Because of television's power to widen pupils' horizons in this manner, many people say it is of undoubted value to education. No matter how remote the subject of the programme may be from the viewer, television can make it accessible. In addition, the resources of programme makers are very much greater than those of the individual teacher or school, so the standard of what is shown – pictures, graphics, quality of information – can be extremely high. Because the result will be interesting, it will also be effective as a teaching tool.

What are they really learning? It can be argued that television, though a useful aid to learning, can be no replacement for direct personal experience. However well produced a programme may be, it leaves the viewer in the role of passive onlooker, receiving experience at second-hand. And what's received is determined not by the viewer's own approach and interests, but by a decision taken many months ago by a programme maker.

Right Video time for two members of the small screen's most enthusiastic audience. Would their teachers be likely to approve of what they're watching?

Far right Walking with music. Anything that fails to match up to the standards of presentation and style that – via radio, TV, or audio or video tapes – surround this consumer will probably be greeted with contempt. But, in the UK at least, schools are often short of money for teaching materials. So how can they manage to compete?

to education?

Some things – moral attitudes, for ex-[am]ple, or an appreciation of literature – [ar]e difficult to translate into television [te]rms. Does this mean that pupils do not [re]ally need to study them? On top of that, [th]e programme maker cannot know the [ne]eds of an individual school, let alone [th]ose of an individual pupil. So the 'lesson' [h]as to be tailored, not to actual circum[st]ances, but to a generalized view of what [th]ose circumstances may be.

A rival system? It can be argued that [w]here the goals of the media and of educa[ti]on differ, the media cannot help but under[m]ine what schools are trying to teach. A [co]mmon aim of education is to produce [pe]ople who are considerate of other people's suffering; a newspaper or TV account of a disaster will frequently highlight the shock and grief of the relatives. A school will urge pupils to avoid violence, to negotiate their

> *'It would be foolish to pretend that the teaching profession has a high opinion of newspapers.'*
> David Lister, news editor of
> The Times Educational Supplement, *1985*

way through arguments, and to put off instant pleasure in favour of later achieve-ment. Advertising, however, concentrates on people having pleasure *now,* while media fact and fiction meet their consumers' need for drama by focusing on confrontation.

'Full of sex and violence'?

The commonest public complaint against the media is probably that they are 'full of sex and violence'. People who think this are likely to add that the matter does not stop there. What worries them even more is the effect that such material, and violence in particular, has on an audience. Much effort has gone into checking whether screen violence really does lead to real-life violence. Over 700 research studies have been published that indicate that it might. But the research methods involved have been criticized, and the whole issue still remains open and hotly discussed.

What's violence? Any discussion on the effect of screen violence on real-life behaviour must start by defining the concept of violence, and this is not as easy as it sounds. The real thing that the researchers are trying to get at is a notion of 'unacceptable'

violence, so their first aim is to work out standard of acceptability. However, people views differ: a viewer who is elderly an timid may be horrified by a screen shoo out in a multi-storey carpark, while he grandchildren remain unmoved. The tele vision series *Dempsey and Makepeace* ha been criticized by the British watchdo group, the National Viewers' and Listener Association, as coming very high indeed i the TV violence league. But a survey showe that more than two-thirds of viewers did n agree; they felt they could handle the leve of violence shown and added they woul miss the programme if it were dropped.

The same considerations apply to se The bare breasts seen in many televisio plays and in 'family' newspapers worr several groups of people: the elderly, th devoutly religious, and some readers wh come from non-western cultures. Does thi

Taboo subject for the press – or a matter of deep public concern? An execution is carried out in a Lebanese street by two Amal militia men.

lean bare breasts should never be shown n television?

howing it like it is? Many would say that ough the 'sex and violence' level accepted y the media is high, it is also necessary. ex is an important (and enjoyable) part of e, and we live in a violent world. People ave a right to know what is going on round them, and they have a particular ght to know if aggression of an unaccept-ble level is taking place, whether it's in the ext street or halfway round the world. It an also be argued that there's a place in e media for the reporting of distressing etails: a close-up of a murdered man's ounds, for instance. Such frankness can ave a healthy effect, since people may be nocked into taking determined action to alt the violence involved.

nothing taboo? Everyone has a 'shock reshold', a point beyond which they find nsational or frank treatment of a subject tally unacceptable. They do not wish to

be upset (or even nauseated) by, for ex-ample, suddenly seeing a picture of a slaughter-house or a man in an electric chair. They may be equally horrified to find they're suddenly watching details of an eye operation during the tea-time news. Readers and viewers feel they have a right to be protected against such distressing experi-ences, which they have not sought and for which they are unprepared. Television pro-grammes can be, and often are, preceded by a warning to sensitive viewers, but warn-ing readers of newspapers and magazines is less easy.

There has to be some consensus on taboo subjects that should be avoided. The difficulty, as always, is deciding just what they are.

Enthusiastic fans greet 'Dirty Den', the handsomely hateful pub-keeper in the BBC's *EastEnders*. The series, which takes a tough, racy look at 1980s life in East London, regularly tops the British audience ratings, and has attracted widespread criticism for its frank treatment of sex and domestic crime.

> *'I believe in showing what does exist and preparing people for the world they live in.'*
> Julia Smith, producer of BBC series EastEnders, 1985

What about the

M any people feel strongly that if there's a case for reducing media coverage of sex and violence, the issue becomes twice as urgent where children are involved. The media acknowledge this; films and television are routinely classified into general and adult-only categories, while there are strict rules about what sort of programmes can be shown at hours when young children are likely to be watching.

Some of the public's disquiet stems from the fear, not yet backed by conclusive evidence, that children will imitate what they see on the screen, with undesirable results in the case of sex and dangerous ones in the case of violence.

But this worry is part of a much more broadly-based feeling that children should be sheltered from the sharp-edged realities of adult life, and that violence, let alone sex, should not be turned into a subject for a child's entertainment.

Just practising? People who in general are opposed to censorship point out that many forms of art – literature and live drama, as well as media productions – help everyone to handle their lives better. They give the reader or viewer a sort of 'nursery slope' on which to practise coping with imaginary events that could, one day, happen in reality.

A child needs to learn coping skills even more than an adult. It is a good thing, the argument runs, that children should be gently introduced to frightening and disturbing ideas through books or television, and thus be allowed to come to terms with them in their own time. Again, violence in children's stories or programmes can, within limits, help readers or viewers, since it defuses their own violent feelings. A further point is that, if anybody thinks children know nothing about sex, they should go into any playground and just listen!

Are they really ready for it? Critics media violence point out that there is difference between a carefully-phased intr duction to the realities of adult life, a full-frontal exposure to it. Since childre experience of life is limited, they may easi misinterpret what they see, and this cou have grave effects on their later develo ment. It can be argued, for example, th constant use of the fictional shoot-out, eve between the good guy and the bad gu implants the idea that disagreements ca only be solved violently. In the world of th action-adventure series, there is little roo for compromise or rational argument, an it is feared that viewers may be prompte to settle their arguments in a similar aggressive manner.

The realities of life: *right,* two children dress up in toy policemen's helmets inspired by TV. *Far right,* boys in the Lebanon pose for the camera with toys that once had other uses.

kids?

Another misinterpretation can, it is claimed, operate at a deeper level. The film cartoon characters Tom and Jerry have been criticized for the violence of their exploits, and the same type of criticism can be levelled at the characters in a highly specialized form of mass medium, the strip cartoon. The common currency here is the sound of blows and cries of pain: 'Crash!' or 'Splat!' or 'Noooooooooooo!' The indomitable Gauls, Asterix and Obelix, knock over rows of Romans, and exchange jokes among the flying fists and knocked-out molars. Some people feel that, in cartoon films and strip cartoons, violence is being degraded, shown as something funny and not quite real. What happens if a child starts treating a friend as Obelix does the Roman army?

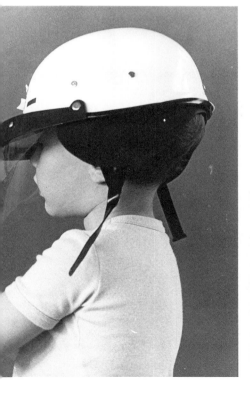

'I find it difficult to believe that the effect of seeing so much violence on television is not damaging to our young people.' Margaret Thatcher, British Prime Minister, 1985

'I don't even touch them, I shake them! It lasts longer that way!'
Obelix the Gaul in Asterix the Gladiator by Goscinny and Uderzo, 1964

Personality plus?

Because they are all branches of the entertainment business, the mass media seldom present audiences with people just as they are. They present performers, larger-than-life figures whose appearances, characters and problems are better and more vividly defined than those of people in the world outside. People who regularly appear on television as 'themselves' are performers too. The relationship between their television selves and their real ones is similar to that between a naked face and one that has been made-up: good – or at least interesting – points are played up, unattractive features are concealed.

Not all the larger-than-life figures built up by the media have the spotlight focused on their positive qualities. Villainy is interesting as well. Without the superbitch and the 'man you love to hate', TV soaps would lose at least half their pulling power, and so would many of the sports that, like tennis or wrestling, put stress on confrontation and on the build-up of personality plus.

This same build-up also finds its way into news coverage. In both western democracies and totalitarian countries news stories thrive on images of good meeting bad; the only difference is that the totalitarian media hero is invariably someone approved of by the current regime. The stories' human subjects are skilfully built up to meet the media's requirements. International leaders from Napoleon Bonaparte to President Reagan and Colonel Qadhafi, have all become suitable subjects for star billing, particularly in the villain's role. It has been argued that this creation of larger-than-life figures, far from enhancing audiences' grip on the reality of the world around them, divorces them from it.

Who wants to be bored? The principal aim of any story-teller is to hold the audience's attention. The strategy employed is to present people who are ordinary enough to be credible, but exaggerated enough to capture the imagination. It can be argued that media presenters are story-tellers like any others, and are merely obeying the first rule of their art: not to be boring. It can also be pointed out that a useful purpose is

> 'People see a piece of fiction as something that's happened in real life. They don't see actors, but real people to whom they can turn.'
> *Russian playwright quoted on BBC 2, 1985*

'She's a superbitch . . . It's great. We think she makes good copy.'
Derek Jameson, British press commentator, on Joan Collins, 1986

Creating a media superbitch is a slow, painstaking business. Here, the camera crew check conditions on the *Dynasty* set as Joan Collins waits for shooting to start.

erved in showing real-life issues in terms f black and white rather than in complex hades of grey. Only the experts, the argu-1ent goes, are equipped to understand the omplexities of, say, an international con-ontation, and they have their own sources f information anyway. For the majority of 1edia audiences, a simplified story that is resented in terms of archetypal heroes nd villains is more truly informative, since presents the matter in a way the audience an understand.

act – or fantasy? Which of these are real eople: Joan Collins, Deirdre Barlow, Terry 'ogan, J. R. Ewing? And what, on television, ounts as 'real': a person playing a character, person playing herself, a person just eing himself?

The most successful characters from television fiction are often treated as 'real' by their admiring viewers, while the actors who create them are shadowy figures, exis-ting only in the context of their creations. When the fictional character gets married, for example, viewers send presents and cards. Meanwhile, the real-life actors are stopped in the street, addressed by their fictional names, and advised what to do about their horrible fictional husbands.

Many people feel that it's worrying to find viewers confusing fact and fantasy in this way. If audiences are persuaded to think fantasy is real, how will they realize that fact, as shown in documentaries or news programmes, is not fantasy? Research, however, has begun to suggest that they can distinguish between the two.

Opposite 'Mad dog' or hero of his people? Colonel Qadhafi of Libya in a pose that would suit the requirements of either role. Photographs taken from a low angle increase the subject's air of authority; few – if any – photographers seem to be allowed to photograph Qadhafi from a vantage-point above him.

Performance rules OK?

T hroughout history, leaders of society – rulers, priests, the military – have felt the need to show themselves to their subjects. Public appearances are an important aid to maintaining power since an invisible ruler is, in the eyes of potential opposition, halfway to being no ruler at all. Today some of these expressions of power have become half-disguised under layers of ceremony: royal tours and papal visits are two examples. But for people whose hold on power is rather less secure, public appearances are still tightly geared to professional success. Politicians and opinion-formers of every sort have a continuous need to show themselves to, and to influence, as many people as possible. Thanks to the mass media, they can now reach audiences vastly bigger than they could on a public parade or a whistle-stop tour. The media are happy to go along with this, since powerful people are automatically news. But does the watching public, composed of subjects, voters or worshippers, lose out?

Good looks, good sense? Using the media effectively is a skilled job. A politician defending a decision needs to be just as much a performer as an actor. In fact some of the techniques involved in, say, performing on television are quite simple: head up, speak out, don't glance from side to side (it looks shifty), and keep it short. But even these simple skills have to be learned, and an increasing number of 'TV schools' exist to help public figures improve their persuasiveness in relation to a media audience. At the same time, there are plenty of professional sources on hand to advise public figures on more general matters, such as hairstyles and voices, while American public life, in particular, shows what skilled dentis-

try can do to make a smile more pleasing

Research has shown that people who look and sound attractive are generally assumed by onlookers to have other positive characteristics, such as honesty, courage and intelligence. (The reality, of course, may be quite different.) It's often argued that a politician's wooing of the public, via the media and media techniques, leads to the same unsafe assumptions being made. Politicians who are good media performers, or indeed just good-looking, are entrusted with responsibilities that they may prove incapable of sustaining. What happens then to someone who is able, energetic and, before the camera, a bore? It can be argued that there is something wrong with a system that deprives society of the services of some of its most useful members just because they sound nervous or insincere, or because their teeth are crooked.

The all-seeing eye? People accept that a television camera's view of its subject is always slightly distorted; for example, it makes people look physically bigger than they really are. But they also say that, when it comes to showing personality, the camera cannot lie. Faults that would escape a newspaper photographer or a live audience are mercilessly exposed on television. Evasions and attempts at bluster are obvious, and so is insincerity: the camera is adept at catching smiles that do not reach the eyes.

It is also true that leaders have always been judged on the way they present themselves as well as on their abilities. The setting has changed, but the principle remains the same: there is no real difference between today's skilled TV-handler and yesterday's demagogue in the market-place.

Opposite (top) The moulding of Margaret Thatcher: as she looked in the mid-1970s, and (inset) more recently. Changes in her appearance have been accompanied by alterations – at least two have been noticed – in the way she speaks.

Opposite (bottom) Hand in hand, Ronald Reagan and his wife Nancy acknowledge supporters' cheers at the 1980 Republican National Convention, at which Reagan was chosen as the party's presidential candidate. Electioneering, American style, has much more razzmatazz than its British counterpart, and is a natural subject for the visual media.

'There is no such thing as the unwinnable interview.'
John Goss, instructor of potential TV interviewees, 1986

'Today's democratic aspirant belongs to the world of soap opera, where what matters is not to stop the show but to make sure it goes on and on.'
Playwright and novelist Frederic Raphael in New Society, 1985

What about

In the countries of the west, a significant proportion of day-to-day news is concerned with industrial relations in one form or another. Stories about strikes hit the headlines, since they are dramatic and also produce dramatic pictures. But viewers and readers also get a constant supply of stories on pay claims, working conditions, health and safety requirements, and all the other topics that arise from working life. Taken together, in fact, these other topics far outnumber the items on strikes.

Opinions differ about the fairness with which the full range of industrial subjects is treated by the media. But certain broad biases are obvious. In Britain, for example, few of the national daily newspapers would in general be likely to present an industrial relations story in a way that was sympathetic to the employees involved. Local papers are more balanced, as is television and radio coverage. But, whoever does the reporting, it's frequently said that the employees' side does not on the whole get a fair hearing.

Talking the same language? Of these two interviewees, which looks the more relaxed, more commanding, less hostile: the factory worker, hunched with hands in pockets on a windy street corner, or the manager, leaning back in an executive chair behind a large desk?

In the eyes of the media's critics, anti worker bias starts with the fact that the employer's side of the story is usually given to the media in the employer's office. However, employees tend to be interviewed in the more taxing conditions of the works yard; out here, noise and the frequent re takes that result, can much reduce the interviewee's self-possession and ability to perform coherently before the camera.

Another charge of anti-worker bias derives from the fact that the manager and the reporter are likely to have a common background, one that has made them both literate and articulate. Quite literally employers may 'talk the same language' as their interrogators. They can understand the questions they're asked, and be able to parry them effectively. Even if they've never studied television performance skills, they will possess the basic confidence that will help carry them through. Many employees however, feel at a disadvantage here, since they lack the type of education that helps the spokesperson on the employer's side to put the management case effectively.

Critics argue that journalists should be aware of this built-in bias and do all they can to correct it. But they have a further graver charge to make as well. By definition all situations involving two sides to a trans action contain the potential for disagreement and confrontation. Confrontation is news, and the most serious claim against the media's treatment of industrial affairs is that they blow up the confrontation aspect out of all proportion to the facts. This is why most people are surprised to learn that strike stories, which are usually presented as attention-grabbers, are in fact outnumbered by other, less dramatic, items of industrial news, and that the number of strikes in Britain has actually decreased over the last twenty years.

> 'What is at stake is the routine processing of information, reports and interviews around one view of industrial crisis. Information that contradicts this is either discounted or ignored.'
> From Really Bad News, by members of the Glasgow University Media Group, 1982

the workers?

'Workers know that they can present their demands 'responsibly' from here till eternity, but it's not 'news' till they go out on strike.'

Paul Hoch in The Newspaper Game, *1974*

So what's important? All the media have a problem over how much they should, or can, say in a story, and how much they should leave out. Television and radio with their short news slots are particularly hard-pressed. Nobody amongst the general public really wants to know the 'whole' story about a situation, and nobody on a reporter's desk would have time to find it out. Many people would say that news gatherers were justified in concentrating on the most important aspects of a story. And they would add that it is pointless to complain about the effects that the desire for an interesting story has on the story's presentation. It is all a case of the 'way we do things here'.

Car workers in the US come off shift. They weren't on strike – so why, in Britain, would the picture instantly seem to spell the message 'industrial dispute'?

Villains

uggers, thugs, yobs, sex fiends and beasts: these are just some of the labels with negative meanings that are put on people by the news headlines. In part, the reasons behind such labelling are practical. They are a kind of shorthand, used to convey coded information in the smallest possible space. But they also express in its purest form the media's preoccupation with creating figures that are larger than life, particularly larger-than-life villains. All communicators know that hate sells newspapers and wins audiences, and not just because villainy is dramatic and therefore newsworthy. At a deeper level, audiences react with great interest to a story that appears to offer them figures they can safely hold in deepest contempt, loathing, or fear. Who these figures are perceived to be differs from culture to culture, and new categories of untouchables appear from time to time: on both sides of the Atlantic, AIDS victims are becoming the latest tragic examples of pariahs-made-to-order. But another social group that is constantly at risk from the media's villain-creating tendencies has been around since society's beginning. It consists of members of any ethnic group

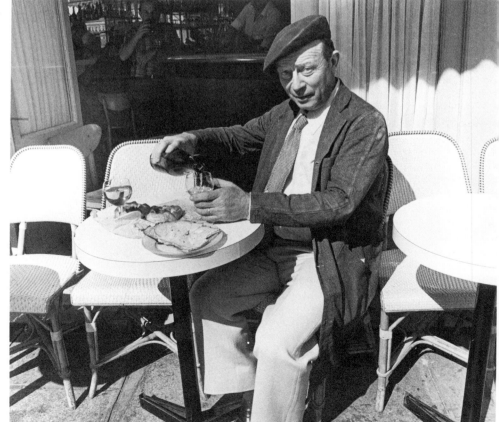

The starting-point of an ethnic stereotype. Like many people in his country, this blameless Frenchman enjoys drinking a glass of wine in a sunny cafe; his German equivalent might be spotted drinking a glass of beer. In the hands of cartoonists and other media workers, these trivial cultural tastes can become principal characteristics of the nation concerned. From there, it's only a step to showing France as a country of lazy, self-indulgent wine-bibbers: prime candidates for villain status if the 'home' culture puts high value on hard work and sobriety.

to order?

ther than the one controlling the medium concerned. Great concern currently exists over the type-casting of these ethnic (and other) groups as artificial 'villains'.

Why not state the facts? Some people point out that people's fears of minority groups in society are no less real just because they may be based on misconception. Old ladies, for example, may live in fear of being robbed on the way to the shops. If they are frightened of members of a different ethnic community, this fear becomes a fact and should therefore be reported.

It can be argued that there is a great difference between ascribing to people crimes they did not commit and crimes that they did. If they committed them, however, there's no reason to hide the fact or to conceal obvious personal details about the criminal. Newspapers feel no need to gloss over the sex of a criminal; why should they feel sensitive about his or her ethnic group?

Fanning the flames? The media's critics point out that the media, in their constant search for villains, too often only see what they want. During Miami's race riots of 1980, for example, a white vigilante group toured around in a car shooting at blacks. A thousand calls of complaint were made to a radio station, but the vigilantes' action was never reported on the air. The only sure way to get on the airwaves, the black community found, was to commit violence themselves: TV newsgatherers were promptly on the spot, alerted by having eavesdropped on police radio.

Bias, it is claimed, is also shown by the media in Britain, where the 'mugger' label (which is not officially recognized by the police) has racist overtones. As commonly used, it holds the message that the criminals are young and usually black, while their victims are white. In fact, street robberies are committed both by and against a wide variety of people, and often the aggressor and victim are both of the same ethnic group. The critics go on to stress that journalists who use ethnic stereotypes to create villains are not just distorting the facts. They are also contributing in a major way to social unrest by deepening suspicions and fears that might otherwise fade. While safeguards exist to prevent the most obvious labelling, it is claimed that these are too easy to get round.

Shrouded against identification, two men are taken to a police station to be questioned. Depending on the crime involved, the appearance of disguised figures like these can be the signal for a hail of abuse from onlookers who – unlike a jury – have judged the case in advance and decided exactly who the villains are.

'Give a dog a bad name and hang him.'
Traditional

'Abandon wogs slum.'
Graffito, Angel Road, N. London, 1986

Are we

A third group of media subjects that allegedly receives biased treatment from newsgatherers, advertisers and other media people is composed of roughly half the members of every country's society: women. In some media contexts, indeed, they get very little treatment at all. A study carried out in the 1970s by a group at Glasgow University showed that the men who were interviewed and named in British TV news programmes outnumbered the women by over ten to one. Two special cases apart, most of the women interviewed were competitors in sporting events or involved in disasters. (The special cases were the Queen and prime minister Margaret Thatcher.) Elsewhere, women tend to be portrayed in the media in one of two main ways, either as home-makers and domestic consumers, or as objects of sexual desire. The headline label that is often applied to members of the first group is 'Mum'; the second usually goes under the label of 'sexpot' or one of its many variants. Considerable concern exists at the moment as to whether this stereotyping of female media subjects is fair, and, if not, as to what its results will be.

Who buys what? In a television commercial, a typical part for a female actor will involve the sales pitch for a shampoo or a brand of packaged food. Male actors have a wider choice of roles open to them: depending on the goods being advertised, they can appear as lorry drivers, top executives, airline passengers travelling business class, fishing enthusiasts, buyers of drinks in pubs, and much else. They may appear in advertisements for male toilet products as well, but they are unlikely to be shown in the kitchen, cooking for the family. In the view of advertisers themselves, this sharp division of roles is perfectly justified. The activity of selling, so

being (s)exploited?

he argument runs, takes place in the world s it is, rather than as some would wish it o be. At the moment, there are more male xecutives and drinks-buyers than female nes. On the other hand, more women than nen carry the responsibility for decisions nvolving the home. It would be a rash dvertiser who deviated too dramatically om these social and economic patterns, ince the advertisement's audience would ail to identify with the situation being isplayed, and the advertisement itself ould therefore fail.

What they all would do? It is also argued hat, given the society we have, women njoy making themselves look as attractive s possible and using their improved ap-earance to improve their social life. A opless model or a 'Page Three' girl is only oing what many women would do if they ared – and if they had the looks for it.

Are women de-valued? Clothes, meals, ome design, children and attracting men: ritics of the media's treatment of women ay that these are trivial subjects compared ith the main issues facing society today. y appearing to confine women to these nd related fields, the media are trivialising alf the members of the human race. Vomen's value, so the media message runs,

is to be judged solely in terms of how they perform in pursuit of such traditionally 'feminine' goals, all of which are geared to pleasing and servicing other people. No matter how much women try to fight free of this limiting role in society, the media keep pressing them back into it.

The media's use of glamour models takes the argument a stage further. Here, critics point out that presenting women as sex-objects robs them not just of their potential social status, but of all dignity as human beings as well, since their bodies are ex-ploited in order to transform male sexual desire into commercial capital.

> *'Women are presented on television, thanks to the distortion imposed by advertising, as if they are something to eat.'*
>
> *Federico Fellini,*
> *Italian film director, 1985*

Opposite Degradation – or a pretty girl showing off her looks?

It's difficult to find pictures of attractive naked or semi-naked men that are aimed at a female audience. The nearest type of male equivalent to a topless model is shown here. But does it really turn women on? And, if it does, do men think its sexploitation?

Beautiful people?

'Real life Dallas is a lot more fun than our Dallas.'

Larry Hagman ('J.R. Ewing'), 1986

All the media in the west are in the business of giving people what they want in terms of stories, information, images. Television and magazines in particular are in the business of providing pleasing images, pictures of good-looking people, beautiful homes, desirable possessions, and delicious food. Advertisers, of course, do the same but with an added urgency of purpose. Their aim is not merely to 'sell' the pictures they present but, through arousing desire and envy, to sell what the picture shows. We are therefore continually surrounded with evidence of the good things that life has to offer. Ordinary people, the message is, can transform their own lives if they try to model themselves on the images they are shown. But is this a realistic aim? And is the evidence presented entirely accurate?

Beyond their grasp? One view is that it is psychologically damaging for the media's consumers to be continuously confronted with images of successful, attractive people and their lifestyles. Their constant presence arouses desires and ambitions in the reader or viewer that often stand very little hope of achievement. In addition, they belittle the consumer's own sense of worth and achievement. A 30-year-old executive, for instance, may feel pleased with his modern estate home and his new family car. But he may think they look drab and dowdy beside the homes and cars of the characters in a lush TV soap opera. On people whose own lives are drab and poverty-stricken, the sight of real or fictitious luxury in the media can have a more serious effect. It may aggravate their depression and deepen their sense of being cut off from a society that prizes the things they lack.

This glorious plum pudding is a triumph of the image-maker's art. In its original form, shown *left*, it demonstrated a very common cooking disaster. One by one, the rest of the currants were carefully inserted by hand.

s that face real? It is also true that many of the media's most beautiful images could never be imitated in real life, since they do not show people in real situations. The glamorous face on a magazine cover has been produced by intricate and lengthy make-up, skilful lighting and very clever photography. Even so, there may be several photographs in the batch taken that make the model look odd, or even ugly; the pictures editor naturally chooses the best one the photographer can offer. But the reader may think she can achieve the same effects every morning before going to work, a conclusion that could be hopelessly wrong.

Goals to aim for? It can be argued, however, that the images presented by the media of a desirable lifestyle widen people's horizons and provide them with goals to aim for in their own lives. It does not matter that the goals are far from realistic, since most consumers are quite capable of translating them into what suits their personal needs and pockets. Few, for example, could afford to fit out their bathroom in marble, but many might well be encouraged to invest in new tiling and a cluster of potted plants.

Furthermore, scaled-down ambitions do not necessarily lead to scaled-down satisfaction. A woman can feel just as good-looking and confident in a 'Dynasty'-type dress bought on a market as in a model creation costing twenty times as much. In many cases too, the media not only set goals but give practical, realistic information on how to achieve them. Fashion, cooking, home-making, cars: these are only some of the fields that are associated with desirable images and that are amply covered by 'how to' magazines of high quality.

Opposite Making sure the image remains perfect: Linda Evans is given running repairs to her appearance between takes of a *Dynasty* scene.

'Put your arms back until it hurts – then you'll know it's right. Now give me a flirty smile.'
Photographer to aspiring model, 1986

Can journalists

Although many aspects of the media's work are controlled by the technology available, there is one media job where the human element still reigns supreme: news gathering. Whatever happens to a story as it goes through the news machine, it still has to be found and recorded by a journalist. In spite of their crucial place in their industry, however, journalists consistently have had a mixed press of their own. Sometimes the public sees them as fearless purveyors of the truth, speedy with their shorthand and honourable in their dealings with sources. But the feeling also exists that 'you can't believe anything you read in the papers'.

Organised chaos on the newsdesk: an accurate portrayal of a newspaper office in the British TV series *Front Page Story*. Within a few hours, the story in the reporter's notebook will be on sale in the streets.

be trusted?

...re we expecting too much? Some people ...ould say that media consumers get just ...hat they pay for. Journalists deal in facts ...d information, but these are only their ...w material. Their primary intention, and ...at of their employers, is not so much to ...ll the truth as to tell a commercially-...able version of it. Added to this profes-...onal goal is another personal one. It is, ...ery day, to produce the day's lead story. ...they are to survive in their jobs, let alone ...t promotion, journalists must also accept ...eir employers' values. If, for example, a ...per is in favour of a certain political ...rty, that is the owner's privilege. By join-...g the organisation, the journalist is de-...aring his or her intention to do nothing ...ovious to rock this particular boat. A ...rther pressure on journalists is time. The ...timate definition of a news story is simply ...at it is new. To bring this new information ... the consumer, a journalist works at very ...gh speed. A story can progress from its ...st beginnings to its final text in a few ...ours. There is no time to cross-check, or ... wait for a more reliable source to come ...ck from on holiday. The story has to go ..., guesses, estimates and all. As a Fleet ...reet sub-editor points out, 'If it's not on ...ne, the best story in the world's no good.'

...power abused? It can be argued that ...though journalists work under undoubted ...essures, the way they try to handle them ...mounts to an abuse of their powers. After ... news event, for example, two journalists ... rival papers might well get together on ...e story. They will decide what aspects to ...ghlight in a complementary way, which ...iotes to use (and how to make them ...lly), and what to say in the all-important

> '*I am in earnest – I will not equivocate – I will not excuse – I will not retreat a single inch – and I will be heard.*'
> Journalist William L. Garrison (1805-1879)

first paragraph. This makes their working lives easier, since neither is going to get a rocket for missing something the rival has featured. But is it fair on both sets of read-ers? After all, each set is paying to read an essentially different account, written ac-cording to different values, from that in the rival publication.

Journalists, however pressured, are still the only channel through which the ordi-nary public can normally have access to rapid information about the world around it. They can approach top people, and insist on getting answers. Within limits, they can indicate whether these answers are credible or not. They can spend large sums of money just on chasing a single fact. In return for the power they are given, they should shoulder the responsibility of passing on the results of their work fully and accurately. Whatever the working difficulties they face, they should not betray the trust society has to place in them.

> '*It's easier and cheaper to take the official view. It's a piece of cake to produce that kind of news.*'
> Greg Philo, director of the Media Monitoring Group, Glasgow University, 1985

Matters of

The photographers strain forward, the cameras whine and click, and rescued survivors from a hijacked aircraft make their dazed way into the public view. It's sometimes argued that press interest of this level can be hard to bear; however, reporters of disasters have found that survivors can be desperate for the chance to talk out their experiences.

In western democratic society, journalists occupy a privileged position. They are not outside the law, but they are outside the system. Their resources, from their telephones and airline tickets to the hours or weeks they can devote to a story, are financed from normal commercial transactions, so they are not answerable to governments. They are not particularly overawed by rank, wealth or social standing, although the presence of any of these in a subject may make them more cautious. Their professional and financial independence is not in fact as great as it appears.

But it is still great enough to give them th[e] freedom to investigate and expose thing[s] that other people and institutions woul[d] prefer to keep hidden.

Protectors of society? There are peopl[e] around today who are free to come and g[o] as they wish and who would be in prison, [if] it were not for the activities of investigativ[e] journalists. Equally, there are people aroun[d] who would probably have died if journalist[s] had not investigated, say, hazardous indu[s]trial practices, and if regulations had n[ot] been tightened up as a result. Often, th[e]

'In his hands correspondence from the field really became a power from which generals began to quail.' Times *man on colleague William Russell at the Crimea, 1854*

public concern?

33

importance of such investigations stretches far beyond the case of the individual most concerned. When, for example, the BBC television series *Rough Justice* brought about the release in 1985 of a wrongly imprisoned man, Anthony Mycock, it was not just Mr Mycock himself who benefited. Society as a whole gained from the knowledge that a wrong had been committed, and that it had been put right.

Again, one of the earliest great figures of journalism, *Times* man William Russell, did not just help Britain's wounded soldiers when he reported on the appalling hospital conditions at the Crimean War of the 1850s. His reports led, via Florence Nightingale's sense of mission, to the foundation of the modern nursing profession.

The most famous journalistic probe in recent years is probably the Watergate case, which rocked America during President Nixon's last years in office in the

> 'The [Watergate] cover-up failed because of a tenacious press and determined individuals in Congress.'
> *Peter J. Mooney and Colin Bown in*
> Truman to Carter, *1979*

1970s. Initially the case appeared to involve no more than a break-in to some of the offices of the rival political party to Nixon's. But as the US press and others dug deeper into the story, the implications of guilt spread further and further, and finally the President himself resigned from office.

How far can you go? While investigative journalists can often be applauded for their tenacity and dedication, it has been said that some are too keen to search for dirt, and that sometimes they find it where it doesn't exist. In their eagerness to dig out a story (and not necessarily one of substantial public concern), they are also accused of harassing individuals and their families and thus causing them unnecessary distress. Criticisms of this sort become particularly acute when the journalist's target has either been bereaved or, in Britain at least, is royal. A further source of criticism turns round the question of how far a journalist is entitled to go when uncovering an injustice. Mycock's release, for example, hinged on a key witness retracting her evidence. 'We were trying to get an innocent man out of jail and her lies had put him there,' *The Times* reported a *Rough Justice* reporter as telling the Court of Appeal. The reporter said that he and the programme's producer had made justifiable threats to her to bring about her retraction, but the Lord Chief Justice, Lord Lane, strongly criticized the programme. And, although it had secured the release of Mycock, the reporter and producer were temporarily suspended from work by the BBC.

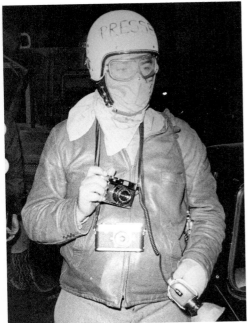

Left Guardian of the truth: a press photographer, masked against the worst effects of teargas, waits to record events during the student riots in France of 1968.

New sports for old?

T he relationship between sport and the mass media used to be straightforward. A cricket match or a ball game took place and it was reported in the press. With the introduction of moving pictures, however, the relationship started to become ambiguous, and it's now hard to say whether the media follow sport or lead it. Thanks to television, sports fans no longer have to attend a match to enjoy it. Many say, indeed, that the experience they get via their TV screen is a superior one. Consequently, attendance at matches is dropping dramatically, with serious consequences for their organisers. At the same time, though, television is creating new sports. When, for example, colour television was introduced in Britain in the mid-'60s, the image of snooker was far from glamorous. However, it was an ideal subject for long-term TV coverage: exciting, visually effective and both easy and cheap to produce. Thanks to television, snooker today is the second favourite sport for men throughout Britain.

Opposite (top) Thanks to television, British skaters Jayne Torvill and Christopher Dean – here shown in their 'Mack and Mabel' performance – delighted millions of people who had previously felt little interest in any sport.

Opposite (bottom) Fans struggle desperately to get clear as a wall collapses at Brussels' Heysel Stadium during the riot of 1985. Twenty-eight people died: a dreadful peak in the violence that is now keeping many spectators away from live football.

Sport-spoiler? It is often said that watching sport on television is a meaningless occupation which does nothing for the viewers' mental or physical health. Instead it just locks them further into a lifestyle where participation in events is minimal and where observation becomes people's only form of leisure activity. Many sports enthusiasts would add that television is also having a harmful influence on the essentials of sport itself. In televised cricket for example, it's the number of wickets captured that counts, rather than the general style of play. Critics of TV sport are also worried about the effect players and viewers may have on each other. Many deplore the way sports personalities 'play to the gallery' represented by a mass audience, and they are particularly worried by the influence bad player behaviour can have on fans.

New heights? The 1980s are a sports-conscious age. More people now take part in sports than ever before, and many of these have had their interest aroused or kept stimulated by television. For those who don't live in mountainous areas, for example, skiing is usually a once-a-year-only activity. However, skiing programmes help keep enthusiasts' interest alive over the other 50 weeks. Skating is a more accessible sport. But here too, television is having a beneficial effect. Outstanding televised achievement like that of Torvill and Dean is spurring skaters on to new heights, and this, it can be argued, is one of the key benefits of the media–sport relationship. The media show potential enthusiasts what the highest standards actually look like, and therefore help ensure that these are maintained.

> *'I know it's just down the road – but you get to see the whole thing if you watch on TV. Who wants to get cold, anyway?'*
> Non-spectator at the Boat Race between Oxford and Cambridge, 1967

> *'I like snooker best. I like the peace and quiet.'*
> Mary Whitehouse, president of the British National Viewers' and Listeners' Association, 1985

Window

M odern communications shrink the world. A radio can carry information where roads have never reached, and television can take its audiences to places and events that in the ordinary way they would never be able to see. Thanks to the media, people today are enormously more informed than they were even a generation ago about most aspects of life. They can take long-distance university courses or, alternatively, learn how to grow better crops. In their leisure hours they can watch entertainments drawn from a wide variety of cultures: Italian opera, American football, Japanese puppet-plays. And they are exposed to new ideas, beliefs, and ways of behaving every time they switch on the television or open a paper.

A distorting mirror? Some critics of the media say that however well-produced a television documentary may be, it should not be seen as a substitute for first-hand experience. The images retained by the viewer are not necessarily those that are of personal value to him or her; they have been pre-selected by the producer, who is working in accordance with the technical rules of the medium. If, the argument goes on, viewers start thinking that they know 'all about', for instance, Indonesia, they are edging themselves into a false position. Safe in the feeling they are knowledgeable, they may lack the impetus to find out more and to discover that the picture they have been shown is of necessity only a part of the truth.

Nature programmes present the problem in reverse. They are widely popular but, as has been sometimes pointed out, they tend to show too much rather than too little. A wild animal spends much of its time in activities that are far from televisual; naturally, sleeping is the main one. The crowded and violent lifestyles shown on the screen are the result of many hours' patient filming; they are therefore a drastically condensed (and over-rich) version of reality, rather than reality itself.

Research has suggested that some people are less, not more, interested in wildlife after watching TV programmes on the subject.

In spite of what will happen to them if they are caught, these French villagers listen intently during World War Two to their illegal radio for news of what the Allies are doing.

'If I see another whale's penis on BBC 2 I'm leaving the country.'
Sunday Times *columnist* Stephen Pile, 1985

36

on the world?

Outside the western world, the mass media sometimes take more primitive – but no less effective – forms. In this Canton street, a large wall poster educates the public in the need to exterminate rats and other pests that threaten health. The lorry, meanwhile, is being used as the setting for a kind of living photograph. The people in it are thieves being displayed to the public before serving their sentences. One of the 'captions' reads: 'Firmly thwart all kinds of criminal elements.'

'I came across a couple of magazine articles on radical women. They wrote it up like a band of maniacs, of course. But at least I knew there were other people . . . who were feeling some of the same things I was.'
Young feminist quoted by Paul Hoch in The Newspaper Game, 1974

Helping people grow? There are many people who would say nothing but good can come of a genuine wish to inform the public, even if the information conveyed by the medium involved may be limited. The electronic media in particular, offer an unrivalled instrument for contacting those who have little access to formal education, and can help them lead more fulfilling lives.

Again, newspapers and magazines not only introduce the public to new ideas. They can be kept and re-read, thus allowing readers to question the findings they present, to test and adapt them for their own use. By acting as a personal library, and one that does not cost much, they can help people's knowledge grow.

Mass

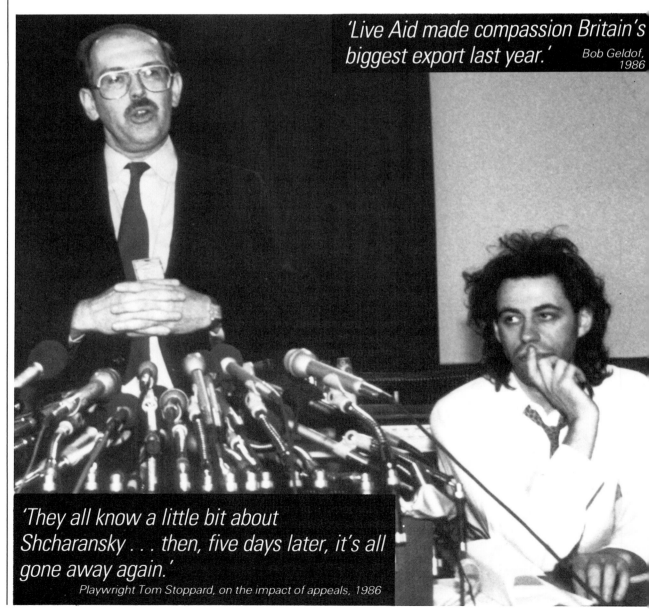

'Live Aid made compassion Britain's biggest export last year.' *Bob Geldof, 1986*

'They all know a little bit about Shcharansky . . . then, five days later, it's all gone away again.'
Playwright Tom Stoppard, on the impact of appeals, 1986

appeal?

Unknown numbers of people are alive today because of a television show that took place in 1985. On 13 July that year, something like 500 million television sets were tuned to the Live Aid concerts taking place in Philadelphia and London. The sum they raised, over £50 million, to help the Ethiopian famine victims also raised the developed countries' awareness of the plight of the Third World in general. In addition, the uncompromising figure of Bob Geldof – outspoken, angry, and commanding huge financial clout – gave a healthy reminder to politicians that the public is equally angry over bureaucratic obstacles to famine relief. Without television and the other mass media, charitable events like Live Aid would find it impossible to make an equivalent impact. When linked with appeals to the public's good nature, the media can exert an extraordinarily powerful force on society. Whether it is a force for good or bad depends on the standpoint of the onlooker.

A force for good? Even the severest critics of the media will admit that, in their campaigning guise, they can do work of immense value. The campaigns do not necessarily have to be linked to fund-raising, either. In the local press, for example, they can focus on consciousness-raising instead, with running headlines like 'Care for that child' or 'Watchpoints for good neighbours'. They can also spearhead campaigns for improved public facilities, such as roads, hospitals, schools, employment prospects; they are equally effective when campaigning against public abuses. They are even effective when linked with campaigns that involve difficult feats of self-denial, such as giving up smoking.

A contributing factor to the power of their impact is the speed with which the impact is made. In today's global village, calamity in the Sahel region of Africa can be beamed direct into living rooms from Seattle to Tokyo. Public response to the sight can be almost as fast, thus ensuring that changes take place in time to save a maximum number of lives. In just the same way, a local newspaper in a developed country can include a new instalment of its 'Good neighbour' series the minute a cold spell sets in. Readers will thus be reminded to offer help to elderly neighbours at the moment it's most needed.

Some causes are better than others? The speed and directness of a media appeal for social change arouse distrust in some people. They point out that it bypasses normal channels such as the democratic parliamentary procedure. A further charge is that the appeal's results, based as they are on emotional reaction, may therefore lack the stability and permanence of changes resulting from a formal decision-making process. Worries also exist about the grounds on which campaign issues are chosen. Some subjects exert a greater pull on the emotions than other. Ill-treatment of animals is an issue that evokes a quicker and more spontaneous response in many British people than, for example, deafness or care of the mentally sick. It is also much easier to illustrate.

On space grounds alone, a newspaper or television channel can only run one campaign at any one given moment. Which of the three good causes mentioned above should it choose if it wants to fulfil its primary aim of earning money and staying in business?

Playing to the audience?

I f you go to an event which you know is going to be reported by the media, your knowledge will affect your behaviour. This is as true of fans at a rock concert as it is of top people with a lifetime of public appearances behind them. When aware of the

> 'Twenty years ago, the mood was tremendously energetic . . . People were always reading about how busy the swinging sixties were, and it affected how they behaved.'
>
> *Sociologist John Nicholson, 1986*

seeing eye of the camera, they will all, to some extent, play to the audience.

In theory, a newsgatherer's job is to remain outside an event and merely to observe what happens. In practice, the event and the media's attention to it are connected. There is an interaction between the two, and sometimes the interaction is so marked that the media may actually, by their presence, cause events rather than merely record them. Coverage of an electoral campaign, for instance, can have a powerful effect on how the electorate actually votes. 'Don't knows' may be swayed in the direction of the party that looks as if it will do well, while its committed voters may be lulled into a state of false security and therefore not turn out. Responsible newsgatherers make their own efforts to 'damp down' or neutralise the effect they have on their subjects. But the really big question is whether the interaction between subject and observer is on the whole a harmful one or not.

Healthy deterrent? In countries where legal punishments are not only reported but inflicted in public, the authorities have no doubt that the link between publicity and the event itself is a healthy one. The aim is to deter potential wrong-doers from committing the crimes that lead to such a punishment. This is also the intention of the judge in a western society who announces an 'exemplary' sentence on a criminal; if the media did not report his decision, its deterrent effect on future events would be completely lost. He is to that extent playing to an audience, and so are the police and military who hope to keep public order by a show – a visible display, reported on TV and by the press – of their presence.

Silence is golden? One area of crime in which the police can often count on the willing co-operation of the media is kidnapping. The help they get is media silence. This is because publicity could, far from

Via the mass media, the world watches as a hijacked plane bakes on the tarmac at Beirut Airport. If reports of hijacks were banned, would hijacking cease?

'We're watching you press bastards. You'll be giving pictures tae the polis.'

Threat made to journalist by Glasgow supporter of Ulster Protestant march, 1985

In an Ulster street, women form themselves into a human barrier to face the troops. The continuing troubles in Northern Ireland have highlighted the question of media cause and effect: the report of an incident there can provoke such strong emotions that further incidents seem sure to follow.

helping the kidnap victim, startle the kidnappers into killing him or her. An argument along similar lines exists against covering airline hijacks. Usually, the argument goes, the hijackers stage their crime to draw world attention to a cause and, with the help of public pressure stimulated by media coverage, to further its progress. If they knew they would automatically be denied publicity, however, they would not commit their crime in the first place.

Just making things worse? Many people, in the media as well as outside them, feel that any situation involving violence, such as a riot, can be made worse by the presence of cameras and reporters, if only because news of the situation's existence will bring further crowds to the scene and thus inflame the situation further. A further problem lies in deciding how far this link between media and events is a real one. Do rioters always intensify their actions when they see the cameras trained on them? Did the carnage at Belgium's Heysel Stadium in 1985 take place because football fans knew half Europe was watching the match on TV? It is very difficult to tell.

Whose freedom, anyway?

Western societies all pride themselves on the freedom of speech and of the press or media that is accorded to their members. Media and public alike, or so the theory goes, have a right to say what they wish, and they will not be penalised for their views. In practice, many people wonder just who it is that possesses this freedom (if, indeed, anyone does). Formal controls over the media exist throughout the western world, but in Britain they are tighter than in many other countries. Some of these controls are exercised through the laws against, for example, libel and obscenity. Others consist of regulations that the media agree among themselves to abide by: the Press Council, for example, rules on complaints about what has appeared in the editorial columns of British newspapers, while the Advertising Standards Authority does the same for advertisements. In addition, both the British Broadcasting Corporation and the Independent Broadcasting Authority strictly control the programmes they broadcast.

Why not just switch off? Some people in Britain say that the British media do not have enough freedom to say and show what they want. Consumers should be allowed to choose what they read, watch or listen to and the choice offered to them should be as wide as possible. If others find items in a liberated press or TV channel offensive, they have only to avoid the channel or publication concerned. In the words of one writer to BBC East TV, 'With reference to those viewers who complained about the lady wrestlers [in mud], they didn't have to watch.'

Necessary controls? An opposing view is that some censorship will always be necessary in order to, for example, avoid presenting children with unsuitable material. The problem is that no two people agree over what is offensive, and for this reason great uncertainty currently exists over what can be allowed to appear in print or on the screen.

A different argument exists over the British libel laws. These are much stricter than, for example, those of the USA. Some people argue that the fear they inspire (and the damages they can lead to) prevents the exposure of social evils and injustices. It is also pointed out that you have to be comparatively wealthy to set up legal proceedings for libel. So is there one law for the rich and another for the poor? On the other hand, it can be argued that the libel laws protect from defamation and embarrassment the overwhelming mass of the population who really do deserve protection

In 1985, a controversy arose over whether the BBC should show a programme it had made on Northern Ireland extremists. The government got involved, and the BBC's governors called the programme off. The BBC's journalists – backed by those on independent television – then went on strike in protest, as shown here. The programme was later broadcast – in an amended version.

Lister intercepts mail!

WINDHOEK: A Windhoek journalist, Miss Gwen Lister, today "accidentally" received a document marked "Top Secret (Uiters Geheim"

CENSORED!

Miss Gwen Lister

a reporter for the Windhoek Observer Newspaper.

Miss Lister told Sapa she had complained about a week ago to the Windhoek Postmaster that her mail was disappearing from her Post Office Box, after it had been sorted into the box.

Yesterday she received a voucher for a registered article addressed to the Postmaster, in her post box.

Believing it was in response to her complaint, she fetched the letter today and discovered

The request, inside three envelopes

"The above address is being used to effect liaison."

Miss Lister said she had handed the document to her legal reporesentatives "for action." — Sapa.

Sugar is hush-hush? In all countries, reporting on matters of national security, such as military plans and defence details, is heavily restricted. In Britain, because of the way the law enforcing restrictions is framed, it is in theory an offence to mention how much sugar a cabinet minister takes in coffee. If this is something a civil servant has learned during his or her work, disclosing it is barred by the Official Secrets Act. It is widely felt that such a law is not only ridiculous, but also makes it easy for civil servants to cover up mistakes that ought to be brought to light. Moves are under way to get it amended.

> 'Beast of Bordeaux proved innocent.'
> *French newspaper headline, libellous under British Law, 1980*

> 'There is never a case for ignorance.'
> *Paul Barker, former editor of New Society, 1986*

So what *did* Miss Lister discover in her mail? At least readers are made aware that South Africa's censors have been at work. There are other censorship systems which are more effective, since there is little to show that censorship has taken place at all. In June, 1986, the South African press was told it would be considered subversive even to leave blank spaces.

Star billing?

'It is proof of British bankruptcy that we seem to feel [the Princess of Wales] is all we have to crow about.' *Julie Burchill*, New Society, 1986

A large proportion of the news presented by the media is about a relatively small number of people, people who are in some way important. Politicians are newsworthy but they are not the only ones. Leading members of society – trend-setters, aristocrats, and the super-rich – are also favourite subjects for a story; so are pop stars and above all, TV actors and personalities. And stories about rulers automatically go straight to the top of the bill. As evidenced by the European press's obsession with the British royal family, the rulers concerned don't even have to be one's own.

Since there are tight limits on newspaper space and programme lengths, some stories always have to be jettisoned when the news is being prepared for communication. The first thing to go will inevitably be a story that's less newsworthy because it deals with a non-important person. News editors operate a mental sliding scale to help them make quick decisions on this point: ordinary people *can* make the headlines of course, but the event that puts them there has to be that bit more dramatic than if a top person were involved. The Queen, for example, gets in the British papers because her train is late; her subjects, however, have to be in a derailment or an aircrash before their travel experiences become news.

Two classes? Critics of the media point out that the amount of attention given to the top sector of society is out of all proportion to that sector's size. By creating two 'media classes' – the automatically newsworthy and the automatically dull – television, radio and the press are working against ordinary people's chances of participating in (and thus helping to control) the media they consume. In addition, a situation is created where the top people

an become increasingly adept at making
se of the media for their own purposes.
overnments do this through a well-
rganized system of 'leaks'. Prominent per-
ormers pay skilled teams of workers to
rganize their publicity. Even private people,
 they lead any kind of public life, soon
earn the names of press contacts who are
lways interested in the chance of a story.
s a result, ordinary people are presented
ith news that is not just *about* top people,
ut often *organized* by them, and aimed at
ther top people as well. Except through
he letters columns of such newspapers as
ave them, the general public's chance of
aking its views known is limited.

re amateurs interesting? The media's
ppetite for stories about top people is, it
an be argued, a completely natural one. In
he west, the media stay in business by
iving the consumers what they want to
ead or see, and what they appear to want
 drama, news of the unusual, and accounts

of people who are glamorous, interesting,
super-competent at what they do. As the
British commentator on the media Jeremy
Tunstall says in his book *Media in Britain,*
'Not many people want their television
screens filled permanently by *amateur*
actors, rock singers, journalists, politicians,
comedians and footballers.' Again, newsgatherers themselves would point out that
giving information about important events
and decisions is a key part of their job. The
people who cause those events and make
those decisions are themselves important.
So it's not surprising that the news columns
are filled with accounts of the actions of
government ministers and top executives.

News is about people who
make decisions. To the
public in each of the EEC's
member countries, some of
these faces will be as
familiar – through the news
– as those of the people who
live next door.

Opposite A top newsmaker
brings some of the less
newsworthy into the
spotlight with her: the
Princess of Wales meets
members of the public.

'Too much publicity can kill you. But the
demand for stories is so great that the
papers just make them up.'
Wham! publicist
Connie Fillipello, 1985

45

The price of the message?

In most western countries, the media are dependent on advertising for a major part, if not all, of their income. In Britain this does not at present apply to the BBC, but both independent television and radio are funded by the advertisements that appear between and during programmes. In the USA another system operates as well: whole programmes can be sponsored by a single advertiser, whose ads, as media people call them, fill all the commercial breaks in the programme concerned.

The production and placing of advertising material for clients is a highly skilled business, and one that can in itself be very profitable. The essence of success lies in matching the ad to the people who are most likely to be activated by it. There is no point, for example, in advertising knitting wool in a computer magazine. There is also no point in advertising an expensive product – luxury cars, say, or round-the-world cruises – in a medium which is read or viewed by people who probably couldn't afford them. The question of the media consumer's income is obviously crucial to advertisers, and has a considerable bearing on their relationship with the media that sell them space or time for their ads.

To be commercially viable, a newspaper can aim to do one of two things. It can go for either an enormous, and relatively poor, readership, or a small, relatively rich one. It is in this division between types of readership that the distinction between 'quality' and 'popular' press is born. Firms that place ads in popular papers know that they will reach a lot of people, even if, individually, these don't have much money to spare. The ad will therefore be most effective for

Buying a newspaper: it seems a simple transaction, but is in fact a complex one. The customers are themselves what newspapers can offer for 'sale' to advertisers thinking of buying space.

'The worst censorship becomes the one you do to yourself.'
Observer *columnist Katharine Whitehorn, 1986*

w-cost products produced on a large scale. ds in the quality press, on the other hand, ill reach a smaller number of rich people, nd will be most effective for the product at is hand-crafted, produced in relatively nall quantities, and expensive.

malign influence? It is felt in some uarters that advertising has a malign in-uence on the media it finances. It is aimed, for example, that advertisers in-uence the editorial content of the medium oncerned by threatening to withdraw their ds if the disputed editorial matter goes in. here is no doubt that this has happened, though cases are obviously difficult to rove. Often the threat to withdraw custom eed never be made; among the unwritten iles media people learn early in their areer is a list of things that can't be said ecause we'll upset the advertisers'. Another harge against the media–advertiser re-tionship concerns the socio-economic atus of the ultimate consumer. It is against ie quality press's interests, the argument oes, to broaden its appeal to people who re less well-off, while the popular press ould also lose out by aiming further 'up-iarket': it would quickly start losing the uge numbers that sustain its appeal to dvertisers. For this reason, it has been aimed that the qualities are deliberately itist in their approach, while the populars eliberately pitch their product to the lowest ossible level of understanding and taste.

he cost of speed? It can also be pointed ut, however, that ads are simply the price iat we pay for having the media at all. A ook costs much more than a newspaper.

But a quality newspaper contains as many words as a book, and is written and pro-duced immeasurably faster. It's the ads that pay for that speed. Again, many ads – in fashion magazines, for example – make a positive contribution to the content and look of the product as a whole.

On the question of advertising ethics, people in the advertising business will point out that advertisers need the media just as much as the media needs the ads. They will also stress that no ad on earth will sell something the public doesn't want to buy. Some backing for this view is provided by the fact that many highly advertised new products fail in the market place.

This gardening cartoon appeared in April – the peak of the plant-buying season – in a London 'freesheet', or local magazine. It was accompanied by a list of local garden centres and garden business advertisements. Freesheets, a relatively new media development, are exactly what their name implies: they are given out free to their public. All their money comes from advertising – and advertisers can be assured of reaching exactly the readers they want.

'I would like to say strongly that we have no wish to see programme content or programme scheduling taken out of the hands of the programmers themselves.'
Kenneth Miles, director of the Incorporated Society of British Advertisers Ltd, in a letter to The Times, 1986

Why don't some

Below Rainy home-going for city gents: their decisions, like those of politicians and other established leaders of society, are a natural topic for the media to report.

The mass media of the western world exist in the main to make money. They achieve their aim by giving their audiences what they want: by showing them and telling them the things they want to see and hear. This aim covers a very wide spectrum of topics, some of which at first glance appear

'The people who bring us the news are mostly male, white and middle-class. Their political position is in the middle of the right. They report events from that point of view.'

Lesley Wood, Campaign for Press and Broadcasting Freedom, 1985

unsettling or indeed distressing. But it doe not cover them all. Critics of the medi have a lot of charges to make against the subjects, and often these are very comple: But one of their most important complaint can be summed up quite simply: 'Wh don't some things get said?' Why, fo example, don't we hear much about gypsie: except in the context of house-dweller objecting to them? Why did it take so lon for awareness of Africa's current famin cycle to reach the general public? (Specia ists in Third World affairs had been discus sing it anxiously for years.) Why can it tak so long for a newcomer on the publi scene – a person, a commercial produc even a charity – to 'break through' an suddenly command the public's attention

Reflecting the real world? Many peopl both in the media and outside them, poir out that the media exist to reflect an report the world as it is. They are nc primarily in the business of pleading specia causes, describing alternative lifestyle: giving full and sympathetic coverage to th views of minority groups. They may indee do all these things, but only in the contex of their basic aim of giving the consumer what they want. If they concentrate on th activities of the main political parties to th near-exclusion of those on the fringe, tha too is a reflection of the world as it is; th main political parties are the ones tha wield the most power and are therefore th most important in news terms. If the view of a minority group – a religious one, mayb – run directly counter to those of the reader ship as a whole, a newspaper has only tw options. These are to ignore the grou entirely, or to present it as peculiar at bes a public enemy at worst. Otherwise th paper would lose many readers and there fore advertisers, and its existence would b threatened.

things get said?

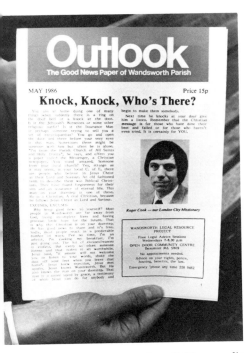

Spreading a specialized message. As *Outlook* acknowledges, most people in Wandsworth are not interested in what the vicar and his committed parishioners have to say. Wandsworth Christians have an outlet for their views in their own paper – but would they have such scope in the wider media world?

Too weird – or too serious? The media of today (though possibly not of tomorrow) cost a huge amount to run, and their critics acknowledge the existence of the financial pressures present. But they argue that people should at the very least be aware that the media cannot help but be enforcers and supporters of the *status quo*.

Genuinely new ideas may get stifled not because they are libellous or otherwise illegal, but just because they seem too weird and outlandish to evoke any response in the consumer at all. Alternative views of minority groups may also get stifled. People prefer to think of gypsies as dirty (since this helps justify thinking of them as 'villains-to-order'); therefore the gypsies' intricate concepts of ritual cleanliness get scant acknowledgement. Again, serious flaws in society may never get reported just because the mere mention of them is too fraught with difficulty, too sensitive, too upsetting. Until recently, for example, the very grave problems of child abuse and incest were hardly ever mentioned by the British media. Then suddenly the taboo seemed to vanish; the problems were brought out into the open and as a result have a much better chance of being tackled. It can also be argued that matters like these are too important to leave to the professional courage of individual media editors and their staffs.

> '*I run my papers purely for the purpose of making propaganda.*'
> Newspaper magnate
> Lord Beaverbrook

A showcase for

E

very country uses its media as part of its foreign policy, to reflect its views on world affairs and to enhance its international image. The ultimate intentions of each state may differ from those of its neighbours: some merely hope to attract more tourists, many are urgently seeking to improve their international trade, and a few seek to interfere more or less drastically with the internal affairs of an adversary nation. But the means at their disposal are common to all: newspapers, magazines, radio. Radio is prominent, since it is the easiest of the really long-distance media both to produce and receive, but the emergence of satellite TV may change this.

Both in the west and in totalitarian countries, governments own or subsidise periodicals or news services that are employed specifically to act as a country's 'showcase'. Positive aspects of the country are emphasized, negative ones explained or left unmentioned. But though these media services represent national showcases at their most sophisticated (and expensive), they are not the only ones. Often presenting a nation in a good light can simply be a question of what is put out on the reception tables at an embassy or a trade function. The best of the newspapers from back home will find a place there, plus the most interesting and attractive magazines. The more vivid publications with screaming headlines will be absent.

Where's the label? Some people feel that the use of the media to promote national interests is wrong, particularly in its subtler aspects. Media deliberately used for national promotion purposes are not unlike commercial advertisements. Ads in a paper or magazine are usually distinguished from editorial matter very clearly indeed. If, the argument goes, 'showcase' publications are clearly labelled as being government owned, readers will know they should take a slightly critical view of the contents. What worries critics is that this sort of distinction is often not made particularly clear, with the result that outsiders may believe the editorial matter is completely unbiased.

An even subtler problem exists where media content is influenced, not so much by governments, but by a whole culture that a government is keen to sell. Thousands of publications exist that are not owned by the US government but which present the 'American way of life' as attractive. Similarly pop music stations of any western nationality have been criticised for pushing western concepts and ideals on eager listeners elsewhere. If a state disapproves of the overt or underlying message broadcast by an adversary nation, how far is it justified in ensuring this never reaches its members by, for example, jamming foreign broadcasts?

Can't they judge for themselves? It can be argued that most readers of a subsidised or government-owned medium are (or become) capable of exercising their own judgment as to the reliability of its content. In addition, foreign broadcasts put out by either neutral or adversary nations may give citizens of some countries their only source of international news. For example, the Russian domestic media contain very little about foreign affairs, and the only way for an ordinary Russian to become more informed about world news is to listen to foreign broadcasts.

Opposite Yellow ribbon welcome: in January 1981, the Americans taken hostage by Iranian revolutionaries at last arrived home to a New York tickertape parade. But the parade and the ribbons celebrated more than the captives' safe return. They also added up to a major celebration, staged before the world's media, of the 'American way of life'.

your country?

'Give me the writing of a nation's advertising and propaganda, and I care not who governs its politics.'

Hugh MacLennan, Maclean's Magazine, 1960

The hardest sell of all?

In a modern revolution, gaining control of the television and radio station is always one of the revolutionaries' first objectives. It is also a primary aim of an invading force in a full-scale war. To either side in the battle, the electronic media are a key weapon in its campaign. Ever since the invention of the mass media, broadcasting and the printed word have been used in wartime to spread information and opinions that will help the side of the broadcasters and hinder that of their enemies. Often the information is false or at least heavily biased, either deliberately to mislead the enemy or to persuade friendly forces to maintain or strengthen their friendship. During World War Two, for example, both the Allies and the Axis used the media – especially radio – to inflate their successes and play down their failures. Sometimes they used the media to play down their successes as well, where news of these would have helped the enemy to counter-attack. Physical control of the media is a crucial aid to ensuring that nothing goes out that is damaging to a country's cause. Almost complete control was achieved by the British government during the Falklands War of 1982. As a result, the world – including the British public at home – received a one-sided and carefully orchestrated view of the war.

The price of victory? It is hardly to be expected that governments would fail to use the media to broadcast information, misinformation and lies in wartime, since during a war it's a case of 'anything goes'. But there is considerable worry about the effect wartime reporting has on the reputation of all newsgathering. Some people point out that the use of the media for what, at any other period, would be seen as a blatantly propagandist purpose, devalues them permanently in the eyes of readers or viewers. If, the argument goes, you can't believe them in wartime, what is there to make you feel they can be believed in time of peace? Knowledge that censorship has existed breeds the fear that it always exists; it just gets better at covering its tracks. It can also be argued that the cover-ups of wartime have a harmful effect on the pursuit of truth once all need for cover-ups is past. For example, most people think that Japan was only defeated in World War Two when the atom bomb was dropped. In fact, Japan had in effect lost the war before Hiroshima, because Allied submarines had completely cut the country off from the oil supplies it needed to pursue hostilities. But the US Navy banned all media mention of submarines at the time, and the ignorance resulting from this ban still persists.

National leaders have many faces, the deciding factor being the side observers are on. Pirate Maggie appeared on the cover of an Argentinian magazine at the time of the Falklands war.

Another face of war: a North Vietnamese child is pockmarked by the scars of bomb splinters. A picture like this one is a powerful weapon in the hand of war's opponents.

Agony is fun? Critics of wartime reporting also attack the manner in which reports are presented. Particularly worrying is the way that death and agony are frequently minimised by the use of semi-humorous turns of speech, often borrowed from the sports field. Television viewers are subjected to the same desensitising process (or desensitise themselves). Phillip Knightley, in his book *The First Casualty,* describes how, during the Vietnam war, the 'hunger of editors' for war details increased as the war went on. Soldiers were filmed in the instant of dying. One Vietnamese, in particular, 'had seen the zoom lens of a sixteen-millimetre converted Auricon sound

camera capturing his last moments of life on film that, if the flight connections worked and the editors back at the network liked it, would be shown in American living rooms within forty-eight hours.'

> **'Don't you know there's a war on?'**
> *World War Two catchphrase, used to justify all breakdowns in supplies, social life, and ethics*
>
> **'Channel 4 is on the air again – to serve the people.'**
> *First words of Philippines TV announcer after anti-Marcos forces capture the state television station, 1986*

The hand of

O n its emergence, every medium of mass communication has in turn been hailed enthusiastically as a 'window on the world'. Among the hopes nourished on its behalf has been the understandable one that presenting the activities, joys and fears of other inhabitants of the globe will lead to greater understanding and friendship among nations. Adversary countries, so the feeling goes, will be demythologized. Their inhabitants will be shown to be people 'just like us', and therefore potential friends. Ill-will between countries will be defused and enmity will eventually cease. How far is this hope realistic?

The whole picture? Given constraints on time and finance, writers and producers cannot begin to show an exhaustive picture of a foreign culture; all they can do is focus on certain aspects that best suit the medium concerned, and hope that these are significant within the culture as a whole. But distortions can creep in, especially if the culture under discussion is a very exotic one. Even the better-documented nations are not immune: thanks to the media presentation of the UK, for example, there are plenty of Europeans and Americans who are sure that British life consists wholly of royal pageantry, strikes, amiable eccentrics, and echoes of the Beatles.

Do New Yorkers relax? It can also be argued that the modern media are helping reinforce, rather than diminish, the national stereotypes that have grown up over time: the amorous French, hustling Yankees, cor-

Inscrutable behind their veils – or just inexplicable? To most western observers, the willingness of these Saudi women to accept their 'invisible' public status seems profoundly puzzling. The modern setting and shopping bags merely add to the bewilderment.

'A little learning is a dangerous thing.'
Alexander Pope (1688–1744) in An Essay on Criticism

friendship?

rect (or crazy) Brits, inscrutable Orientals and so on. The camera only sees what it's pointed at, and producers have a strong temptation to point it at something that will make sense to the ultimate audience. A relaxed New Yorker or an expansive city gent from London are, for many television viewers, almost a contradiction in terms. Yet understanding can only start when stereotypes are seen as the exaggerations they are.

A further problem for journalists and producers is posed by the 'resident' stereotypes of their own cultures. When, for instance, Presidents Reagan and Gorbachov met in 1985 for their fireside summit at Geneva, the western media were bemused by the way Mrs Gorbachov did not match up to their conventional western image of a Communist top lady, that is, dumpy and dour. Deprived of their usual frame of reference, newsgatherers therefore fell back on showing her as they would a good-looking woman of the west: all the talk was of her clothes and of the 'coffee morning' relationship with the US president's wife.

Too hard-hitting? It can be argued that the portrayal of foreign cultures can actually make international relationships worse. A hard-hitting programme on, say, the treatment of women in Arab or African countries can shock westerners into feeling that all Arab men are tyrants and all African cultures are barbaric. Too often, extending the hand of friendship can come under the 'sensitive' topic heading, only to be treated with kid gloves.

Geneva, 1985, and one of the meetings between the US and Russian First Ladies. The media loved it – but how much did we really learn about either Raisa Gorbachov or her US opposite number?

'Nation shall speak peace unto nation.'
Motto of the BBC

Finest in the world?

Opposite (top) Padlocks and prizes in the British game show *The Price is Right.* The game show concept is one of the classic American contributions to television fare worldwide.

The British are fond of saying that their television is the finest in the world. In fact, most of them have seldom seen television anywhere else, or are able to understand it if they do. What they really mean is that the object of their admiration has a uniquely 'British' voice, and that this voice is superior to anything produced anywhere else in the English-speaking world, particularly in the USA.

Sincerest form of flattery? Critics of the starry-eyed attitude of the British to their own television point out that the BBC and the IBA are as happy as anyone else to achieve high ratings for their productions. As a consequence, they are under continual pressure to show a proportion of programmes that will appeal to as large an audience as possible. 'Large', in British terms, is expressed in tens of millions. In early 1986, the BBC's top-rating programme, the urban soap *EastEnders,* was achieving audiences of 23 million, while its opposite number on the independent network, the long-running *Coronation Street,* notched up viewing figures of nearly 18 million. Both these series appear home-grown to the core: *EastEnders,* as its name implies, deals with life east of London's Tower Bridge, while *Coronation Street* performs a similar task for the industrial belt of Britain's northwest. But the soap opera format itself is American (US radio had them in the 1930s) and transatlantic soaps like *Dallas* also command massive support from the British viewing public.

Another highly popular form of television programme in Britain is the game show. But this too is American in inspiration, as is the fast-moving action drama. Even the heroes of British TV can have something in common with their US opposite numbers: outsider and high-minded ex-con Terry in *Minder* is not very far removed from earlier hero figures like the Lone Ranger of pre-TV westerns.

British television has agreed a limit on the amount of foreign television that it imports and shows to British audiences. But the imports – which, because of the language problem, tend to be transatlantic – include some of the most popular programmes seen on television. It can also be argued that, far from cultivating its own unique voice, British TV is over-keen to show, through imitation, the sincerity of its admiration for US production standards and viewing figures.

Good ambassadors? Defenders of British television acknowledge the heavy debt it owes to the American media. However, they point out that Britain can nonetheless boast more than enough television material to justify its claim to both its distinctive voice and high quality. There are the current affairs programmes like *Panorama,* and the serious dramas, series or one-off, like *Jewel in the Crown.* Many costume dramas also qualify, with *Upstairs, Downstairs* being one of the most popular, while the soaps like *Coronation Street* have their well-deserved national (and international) following. And no-one can deny that British television makes the most of the two unique assets it continuously has on hand: the home-grown dramas of Shakespeare, and the activities of the Royal Family. The British programmes that go abroad hugely enhance Britain's reputation for quality programme making. It has been asked, however, whether they really act as good ambassadors for the country they represent.

Opposite (bottom) Dame Peggy Ashcroft and bearer in *Jewel in the Crown,* one of the most highly-praised British TV productions of recent times.

'Coronation Street . . . *has provided Granada with the biggest bulk sales coup in TV history: 1,114 episodes to a station in Saskatchewan, in Canada.'* The Times, 1985

'Whether a costume drama/ Royal ceremonial/zany comedy view of Britain is really a useful export from modern Britain is a question easy to ask but hard to answer.' *Jeremy Tunstall* in The Media in Britain, *1983*

The media

There is no doubt that, whatever use is made of them, the world's mass media are successful, popular and highly profitable. They have enormous power, to be wielded for good or ill, and the portion of this power that is conferred on their owners is a magnet to those that can afford it. This situation has obtained for something like a century, dating from the time when the introduction of cheap paper made of wood-pulp allowed newspapers to reach out for huge, as opposed to merely influential, audiences. Since then further technological innovations have brought further dramatic changes, and more innovations and changes are now on the horizon. What effects are they likely to have on the media as we know them? And will the effects be desirable ones?

Do we deserve what we want? It's claimed in many quarters that the mass media are too powerful. It is true that the most vociferous critics on this score are often those – politicians, clergy, teachers, parents – who have most to fear from a rival source of power that relies on techniques that they're unable to use. For that reason, at least some of their criticisms may be suspect.

However, it is also true that a bad effect of the media's power is to restrict consumers to a comparatively narrow diet of experiences (all by definition second-hand), facts and views. By definition too, these views will be 'received': the opinions most likely to appeal to a majority of those at the audience end of the medium in question. It can indeed be argued that, by being ready with a received view on anything and everything, the media are relieving consumers of the need to think for themselves. And it can also be argued that whatever changes may

Right The shape of things to come? Two parabolic television antennae – commonly known as backyard dishes – are set up to receive satellite transmissions. As dishes (which can receive programmes from both home and abroad) become more common, the amount of programme choice open to viewers will expand dramatically.

'Recently, [the press] has seemed at one of its lower ebbs. But – thanks to the new technology – the tide may yet turn again, against monopolistic unions and monopolistic proprietors.' New Society, 1986

we deserve?

overtake the media in the remains of the twentieth century, they will continue to operate on the basis of giving consumers what they appear to want. Whether we deserve this is another matter.

Wanted: newspaper (going cheap) It would be easier to defend the media from all the charges that are levelled against them if they were, in fact, *better* at giving the public what it wants than they actually are; if they were more responsive to the needs of people with widely divergent or minority views. A greater gain still would be if it were more widely possible for such people to set up and run a publication or a TV or radio station of their own.

Where the published media are concerned, such accessibility has been ruled out even in the very recent past by the enormous costs of running newspapers and other publications. But with the development of computerized production and printing techniques, costs should soon start to fall. This means that newspaper owners of the year 2000 will not have to rely as heavily as they do now on advertising revenue, and this in turn will free them from the need to put circulation figures before all else. Small, specialist readerships will become viable.

Again, the only thing that prevents greater access to TV air waves by relatively small, low-budget operators is the tightly-controlled licensing system that governments operate. Here too it seems possible that at some point in the fairly near future these controls will be relaxed, as has been the case with radio waves in many countries. When, however, all these and other developments come about, it will be for a new generation of media operators to find out whether the public really wants a wide range of minority-oriented media, or whether the older mass-market media will still retain their hold.

'I look around for some old-fashioned paper to draw on and realise that there isn't any.'

Cartoonist Mel Calman, on moving to the new Times *premises at Wapping, 1986*

Reference

The development of the mass media

1200 (approximately) The Chinese of the Southern Sung dynasty invent the technique of printing on paper by assembling woodblocks carved with the characters required.

1438 (approximately) A German printer, Johann Gutenberg, re-invents in Europe the process of printing with moveable type. Until this point, books could only be printed by carving the words of a whole page on to a woodblock; now, however, text can be processed as quickly as a printer can assemble individual letters into words or sentences. Mass production of printed matter becomes possible.

1476 William Caxton sets up a Gutenberg-type press in London.

1594 Printers in Cologne, Germany, produce the first publication ever to appear repeatedly and regularly: a news summary (in Latin) called the *Mercurius Gallo-Belgicus*. Thanks to its distinctive publication pattern, the *Mercurius* is acknowledged as the earliest ancestor of the modern newspaper and magazine.

1600s Wars and unrest in Europe and Britain encourage the production of regular news journals, and thus bring the first journalists into existence.

1805 In Britain *The Times*, then still a very young paper, scoops the world and secures one of the greatest journalistic triumphs of all time by reporting the victory at Trafalgar and the death of Nelson before the British government could get out its own announcement.

1800s (early) Newspaper production is speeded up by the introduction of printing presses powered by one of the main energy sources of the Industrial Revolution, steam.

1840 The first positive-negative camera is invented by English scientist W. H. Fox Talbot.

1845 The first public telegraph line is opened between Baltimore and Washington in the USA. The message is transmitted by electric current in the 'dash-dot' code developed by Samuel Morse. For the first time, the instant transmission of complex information over long distances becomes practical.

1854 William Russell of *The Times* horrifies Britain with accounts of conditions at the Crimean War.

1861 The last British tax controls over the press are abolished.

1876 Scots-born scientist Alexander Bell sends the first long-distance message by voice, via the telephone he has invented.

1877 With his phonograph (ultimate ancestor of the record-player), Thomas Edison invents sound recording.

1884 Ottomar Mergenthaler, a German immigrant to the USA, invents the Linotype machine. This, which automates the type-setting process, speeds up newspaper printing still further and makes it much cheaper. (Linotype machines have been in general printing use until very recently.)

1880s Paper made out of wood pulp, rather than the more expensive rags, comes on to the world market. Periodicals can now be printed both cheaply and in huge numbers.

1895 The French brothers Auguste and Louis Lumière open the world's first cinema in Paris, using the camera/projector they developed from

...e camera/ciné viewer developed in the 1880s ...y Thomas Edison.

...895 In Italy, Guglielmo Marconi transmits the ...rst radio signals, from his house to the garden. ...1901, the radio age is formally opened when ...e sends a signal in Morse code across the ...tlantic.

...925-6 Scotsman John Logie Baird makes the ...rst long-distance transmission of a moving ...icture and demonstrates his television system ...a mechanical one – to scientists. Later, his ...stem would be briefly adopted by the BBC.

...926 The British Broadcasting Corporation is ...et up.

...928 Colour television is first demonstrated, ...gain by Baird.

...934 Radio brings British royalty into ordinary ...eople's living-rooms, when King George V starts ...e tradition of Christmas broadcasts.

...936 The BBC begins the world's first public ...elevision service; in 1937 it drops the Baird ...stem and changes over to an electronic one.

...941-2 Radio broadcasts made by wartime prime ...inister Winston Churchill reach 70 per cent of ...e British population, an enormous audience ...gure.

...969 The world watches television pictures of ...e first Moon landing.

...969- The escalation of violence in Northern ...eland raises major questions on the role of the ...edia in relation to the events they report (or ...ause).

1972-1974 The Watergate affair; US newspapers, particularly the *Washington Post,* play a prominent role in the investigations that followed the Watergate break-in.

1985 The British government eases restrictions on ownership of parabolic TV antennae, or 'dishes', essential to private reception of satellite televison.

Reading and viewing

Bad News (1976), *More Bad News* (1980; both Routledge & Kegan Paul), *Really Bad News* (1982, Writers & Readers), all by the Glasgow University Media Group. Famous radical series that opens up wide areas of criticism against the media. Spiky and entertaining.

Broadcast Near-weekly journal, published by International Thomson Publishing. Glossy trade paper for media people; to outsiders, offers considerable insight into the business.

Campaign Weekly journal published by Haymarket. Similar format to *Broadcast*; aimed at the advertising business.

Channel 4 News Makes a deliberate effort to break away from one-sided reporting of the type attacked by the Glasgow Media Group and others.

Company Monthly magazine, published by the National Magazine Co. Probably the most socially aware of British magazines for young women. Thoughtful discussion of key social topics (the media included) is regularly featured.

The First Casualty by Phillip Knightley (André Deutsch, 1975; revised edition Quartet Books, 1982). Deals with the role of the war correspondent 'as hero, propagandist and myth-maker'. Engrossing (but at times distressing) reading. The 'first casualty' of the title is truth.

The Listener Weekly journal, published by BBC Publications. Deals with the whole range of media issues. Highly informed, provoking, often very funny. The issue of 24th April 1986, on changes facing the newspaper industry, is essential reading; local libraries may have it on file.

Local TV and radio news Always listen to any accounts of events you have personally experienced. How does your experience differ from that presented by the journalist?

The Media in Britain by Jeremy Tunstall (Constable, 1983). Solid going (plus plenty of statistics), but excellent. Huge list of sources for further reading.

New Society Weekly journal, published by New Society Ltd. The magazine for informed fact and opinion on all social aspects of late twentieth century life (plus frequent discussion of the media's contributions to them).

The Newspaper Game – the Political Sociology of the Press by Paul Hoch (Calder & Boyars, 1974). Well-argued case for the prosecution against the media as Establishment tool. Impressive amount of evidence produced; unfortunately, no index.

The Politics of Information by Anthony Smith (Macmillan, 1978). A concise and lucid examination of a range of media issues (the book is an essay collection). The final section on the interaction between media content and media technology is an outstanding introduction to the subject.

Uninvited Guests: the Intimate Secrets of Television and Radio by Laurie Taylor and Bob Mullan (Chatto & Windus, 1986). Latest insight into what viewers actually think. (They're by no means as easily fooled as some would have us believe.)

ndex

Credits

The author and publishers
would like to thank the
following for their kind
permission to reproduce
copyright illustrations:

Aldus Archive: 10, 29
Aldus Archive/Imperial War
   Museum: 36
Aldus Archive/Library of
   Congress: 4
Associated Press: 40
Simon Burder: 49 (both)
Camera Press: 41, 53
Central Television: 57 (top)
Sally and Richard Greenhill: 1
   12–13, 13, 16–17, 24, 46

IDAF: 43
Popperfoto: 5, 7, 21 (bottom),
   23, 25, 30, 35 (bottom), 44
Betty Rawlings: 58–59
Rex: cover, 21 (top), 26, 27, 42,
   45, 48, 57
Rex/GAMMA: 33
Rex/SIPA: 8, 17, 18, 19, 28, 32,
   35 (top), 37, 38, 51, 52, 54, 55
Southside Magazine: 47
Syndication International: 15